CW00400140

Don't Organise My Tears

Reflections on Bereavement

A J Bailey SDB

illustrated by Mavis Bates

Don Bosco Publications

Published by Don Bosco Publications 2000

Don Bosco Publications
Thornleigh House
Bolton
BL1 6PQ
01204 308 811

ISBN 0 9538991 01

Printed and bound by Alpha Printing, Bolton

To Mum
1912 - 1992
in gratitude

Contents

Introduction

'Don't Organise My Tears' may not appear to be an invitation; but surprisingly enough it is an invitation to get involved in the grief of others. Not in any interfering way, but by sympathy and compassion. The verses in this small book express my involvement in the grief I witnessed in the lives of others. All grief is unique, I cannot know what you are suffering. However I found that when I attempted to express in verse my grief in seeing others grieve, it helped me cope. It is in the hope that they may be of help to others that these verses are published.

Most of these verses were written at a time in my life when I became strongly aware of the bereavement suffered by many. I was coming to the end of my time as Headteacher at our Salesian Comprehensive School in Bootle and I was tired. About the same time my mother died. Her death affected me more than I had anticipated. I found that attending funerals of the parents of pupils, or pupils themselves was always a very moving experience. Never underestimate death. Writing verses seemed the only way I could cope with the weight of bereavement. At this time I also helped, as a priest, in St Matthew's parish in West Norwood, London. Here I became aware that while people expected me, the priest, to help them cope, I was so often struggling myself with the mystery of bereavement.

The verses begin with the effect the sight of a young woman had on me when she bravely stood at the funeral service to pay homage to her father, an image that was a source of great strength to me. 'Elaine' and 'Iain's Father' represent the way children suddenly find they are faced with a seemingly impossible burden of grief. 'James' tries to capture the way a school feels when one of its pupils dies, James was a sixth-former who died of leukaemia just when we thought he was recovering after long years of painful treatment. 'Mary' tells of the more tranquil passing of a much-loved mother, and a church full of incense and the sun shining.

'Funeral of a Deacon' attempts to be a way of expressing appreciation of one who had helped me during my mother's funeral and how each person, at a funeral, brings their own memories of similar days of grief. 'Howard's Funeral' expresses the deep feeling of inadequacy at the sight of children suffering the loss of their father. I had to write something when Philip Lawrence died so tragically because his death typified for me the total sacrifice of a genuine teacher. The 'Children's Holocaust Memorial' was the result of a visit to Jerusalem and the feeling that we still need to learn to protect children from a similar fate. 'Mother' and 'Caring for Mum' reflect on the way bereavement is part of a process and often cannot be separated from a period of care, a painful but often rewarding accompaniment of a sick parent. 'Sharer in Suffering' attempts to make the point that involvement in the sufferings of others can change us and put many priorities into perspective. It refers to the way a friend of mine was changed quite radically after he had counselled victims of a disaster. 'News of Her Death' was the result of a friend of mine who, coming home late on Christmas Day, found a note on the board to say that a great friend of his had died. I make no apology for a frequent reference to 'Memories' for they are so important in the grieving journey. 'At My Funeral' is by way of light relief lest we take ourselves too seriously and because many of the funerals of my Salesian brothers have been joyous occasions of celebrating the good things in their lives. The last few verses attempt to capture common themes of bereavement, the feelings of being Miserable, Grieving, Out of My Depth, Compassion, Sympathy, and that ambiguous feeling of not wanting people to organise your tears but at the same time needing them. The final verse 'Perceive New Colours' is written in the hope that if we learn compassion for our brothers and sisters we may help to bring new colour into their lives and our own.

I am so grateful to Mavis Bates for agreeing to illustrate these pages. I feel her delicate and sensitive interpretations are so much more than illustrations. Her most original 'take' on each verse serves as an encouragement to the reader to explore the subtle body language of grief and help us translate the words which so often awkwardly but painfully express need.

Tony Bailey

Tribute to Her Father

Phil's brave daughter stood to praise her father.
Spoke from her heart in words that moved me.
Spoke for herself, and spoke for her family.
Steady her voice as the priest standing by her.

Clear her voice, clear as the love she celebrated.
I listened and was moved near to tears.
Why do I want to cry when a girl is brave?
Speaking love to him she speaks strength to me.
Phil gave her life; Phil gave her love.
In death he hears her prayerful praise.

I prayed selfishly for tears to win.
My tears more to me than grief.
I listen and my tear-needs cease.
Drowned in the sound of a daughter's hymn.

Caring for Mum

Days long with caring, all Saturdays.
Nights dark with confusion, little sleep.
Vocation of listening, stories of olden days.
Mother and daughter, love goes deep.

Years spent together, love grows.
Service of dependence, hard to accept.
Praying together, God knows.
Service of love, never regret.

What mystery of love in this!
A mother should be mothered
And daughter life should miss
But life's deeper joys discover.

Elaine

Another funeral today, Elaine's Mum died.
Elaine is fifteen, her Dad dead but a year.
"What can I say to Elaine?" I sighed.
Nothing! And I watch her tears, my fear!

The deacon prayed well, he was sincere,
Familiar prayers for this unfamiliar day.
I listen and his prayers I hear,
But my mind is far, too far away.

Has any child the strength to bear this cross?
Snatched from childhood to act out a part
For which much older people feel at loss.
Loving Lord, where is thy heart?

Know I'm Grieving

Leave me, know I'm grieving.
Please see the pain within me.
Don't tell me how I'm feeling,
Don't diagnose deceive me.

Hold me. Feel me grieving.
Your arms have meaning for me.
They reach me, not deceiving,
Anchor me, my mooring.

Need me. Want me grieving.
Don't leave me, go unheeding.
Don't tell me time will heal me,
Feel this present need within me.

Hear me. Heed me grieving.
Leave me tell my story.
Look at me! Your sympathy!
Our friendship? I'm imploring!

Guide me. Lead me grieving.
My life has lost all meaning.
My compass be until I see
The value in my keening.

Sharer in Suffering

Privileged to share in suffering.
To feel in depth the grief in men,
But then to think you walk away,
Back home to be immune therein.

Immune? There is no shield from suffering.
Once seen. Once felt. You change.
You go away, but see again, again;
Their wounds of grief still festering.

Your eyes have seen, have focused in.
They never see the same again,
For they have seen beyond the ken,
Of selfish human reckoning.

Treasure then true reckoning.
Let others fight for lesser things.
Their price, their wealth, their dividend
Grief's brokenness won't mend.

Iain's Father

"Let not your hearts be troubled.
Neither be afraid."
The Scottish minister prayed,
His accent strong.
I prayed but my heart was troubled
Deeply I sighed
Iain's dad but forty-five.
For Iain afraid.

"Let not your hearts be troubled
Neither be afraid."
Like a chorus played.
Accent strong again.
Of course my heart was troubled
Troubled for the family
Suffering plain to see
I was afraid.

"Let not your hearts be troubled
Neither be afraid."
For Iain's Mother prayed.
Held in my arms.
Arms round Iain held
Held in his grief
My words but brief,
"Look after Mum!"

James

Silence in our school today, questioning?
James has died, feelings high, think of him!
Too young to die, too good to lose,
Too weak to cry, too harsh the news.

It's funeral day, St James' Church, crowding in,
His family, his football team, all friends for him.
We say good-bye, we fight the tears,
We pray in sighs, express our fears.

His days in school, such memories!
Just think of James, all good things his!
He had high hopes, his future bright,
On football field, in family, all lost to sight.

Our Sixth Form weep, a school must grieve.
Not walk alone, as church we leave.
James was our friend, we're lost today.
Will this pain end? Take grief away?

Our children show when death arrives
The depth of feelings in their lives.
Eyes filled with tears, no tears to hide.
They conquer fears. They weep in pride.

Lord we thank you for your gift of school.
Some days we wonder, "Worth it all?"
Now we see the point of it. The child mature!
Privileged as part of it. The strain endure.

Funeral of a Deacon

Terry, deacon, walked with me;
Behind my mother's hearse that day.
He, strength had been, prayed with me,
Three years ago, his strength my stay.
This memory came back to me,
Walking now behind his hearse.
In funerals, when dear friends die
Strong memories revive.

Under that cold dark winter sky,
Shadowed by a sad yew tree,
I gazed across the waiting grave
At faces lined in agony.
I saw deep love of Terry there,
Sob-evident in every face.
Felt them wince at memory's stare
Past in their present grief they taste.

I'm sure I'll not forget this day;
Dark sky, sad tree of memory.
Dear friend of ours returns to clay.
A mother's grief too clear to see.
Each felt for him, each cried for her,
Their own deep loss, a mother's plight.
Each troubled too by memory's stir,
As parish, friends, in grief unite.

Terry, friend, has walked with you,
In your joys, with your grief.
Your troubles too he listened to,
His kindliness ran deep.
His death you feel dismayed in pain,
Incredulous in loss of him.
Cherish rather all the gain
His life, in gifts, has been.

Mary

The sun shone bright that Thursday,
The day we buried Mary.
So much there was that shone that day,
The day we buried Mary.

'Star of the Sea' shone brightly,
A church so full of piety.
Praying there for Mary,
May she rest most peacefully.

The family shone brightly,
Grief-filled but prayerfully.
Praying for their mother there,
Their faith shone peacefully.

A crowd filled 'Star of the Sea'
Showing that they cared for her.
Caring in their praying there,
Requiem for Mary.

Three priests incensing then,
Finale for Mary.
Smoke goes up like people's prayer,
Praying for Mary.

Howard's Funeral

Mother, wife and little children!
Today is Howard's funeral day.
Speechless me, I gaze at them,
Lost for words to say?
Prayers I can say, officially
And hide in missal words.
I really need much more from me
My heart cries to be heard.

Helen, age three, I had baptised
That happy Easter night,
Recalled today. Her dad had died,
Too young to understand her plight.
Funerals, priest in control,
But inwardly all agony.
Their pain tears at my soul,
Composed for them to see.

Philip Lawrence

Requiem for him
Who intervened.
Children in need,
Teacher to the end.

Presence to protect
In front-line found.
Presence with us yet;
Example sound.

Listen now and learn!
Lesson in life's cost.
Help our young discern
Values we have lost.

(Westminster Cathedral, 22nd. January 1996)

Don't Organise My Tears

Don't organise my tears for me.
Don't tell me when to cry.
Don't tell me how it's hurting me.
Don't orchestrate my sighs.

My grief is confidential,
A secret known to me.
Don't torture me with kindness
To prise this secret free.

You cannot see inside of me,
Can't measure me for pain
Stop telling me how hurt I'll be,
You diagnose in vain.

By all means stand the side of me,
I need someone who's near
Don't walk away, no words to say.
Your message is quite clear.

Be patient with this side of me,
Not gracious in my grief!
You've seen some better days with me,
Time now to grit your teeth.

Don't hesitate to smile with me,
All moments are not sad.
Revive a few fond memories
Of better times we've had.

You know grief makes a fool of me,
So humour me awhile.
Be patient with the fool you see,
I'll tolerate your smile.

And if you have to cry with me
You won't offend my tears
Our confluence of tears can be
The union of our fears.

At My Funeral

At my funeral please smile
Think of the stories we would tell.
Please celebrate my life for me
I may be dead but I am well.

Remember how you laughed with me
Enjoying other days,
Hearing my poems read by me.
Read one now in your own way!

Please play some tunes you know I liked,
No mournful melodies all grim.
Jazz band indeed would be ideal,
Please sing for me some cheerful hymn!

And afterwards please reminisce.
Talk of the good times that we had.
Make sure you find some time to laugh.
Don't let my going make you sad!

Mother

Remembering the changes of her years,
Dependence become responsibility.
From tears of a child to adult fears,
She always saw her child in me.

Her critical eye while I decide
Her mothering until the end.
Never sure how to confide,
Knows, but does she comprehend?

Grateful now for needs well met.
Long days seeming no success.
Bereavement now, but no regret,
She calm completes my happiness.

Vision bright for tired eyes,
Happiness and she can see.
Appreciates her caring child
Memories she leaves to me.

Seen my Brother Suffer

Lord I've seen my brother suffer,
Seeing mother fade in pain.
Spirit strong in family strong,
But life still ebbed away.

How she changed; appeared to change.
Her strength remained apparent.
Sorry not for self but them.
Why should they see her suffer?

Father, son, to care committed,
In their own way, nursing her.
Reluctant she surrenders care,
A mother's greatest privilege.

What mystery of family love,
That roles might be reversed.
That son can now a mother be,
And husband be a nurse.

Now Lord her day of joy has come,
Freedom from her pain; their care.
Grateful for her loving son,
Grateful for her husband there.

They too feel some share of joy.
Her vanishing well ended.
The new phase of their lives begins
When memories are tended.

Sympathy

Within your pain there's pain for me
I suffer too, that's sympathy.
Friendship endures, as joys we share.
When suffering comes I'll still be there.

Not there to add my pain to pain.
By saying words, just words in vain.
There more to listen, carefully,
To feel your pain as pain in me.

No need to thank me for my time,
Or feel obliged when I am kind.
Just know this friend, as friend remains,
To smile until you smile again.

Until you find your feet again,
Can walk away from present pain.
I'll limp with you quite cheerfully,
Pain shared by two, that's sympathy

Memories

We came to town to bury Mum.
I came with dreams to realise.
I gazed, but with new eyes,
Same town, but in new guise.

Each scene reminded me of Mum.
She spoke to me on every street.
Her history was there to see.
Old friends she'd come to meet.

Each view spoke to me of her,
Her church, her shops, her ways.
Her stories stalked on every street.
My eyes blest with her gaze.

The town that day was changed for me.
Changed by the life she knew
Her years rolled into one that day
I listened, watched come true.

There are those days, glad vision days,
When heart persuades the mind,
And eyes are guided by the past,
Life's truth in death you find.

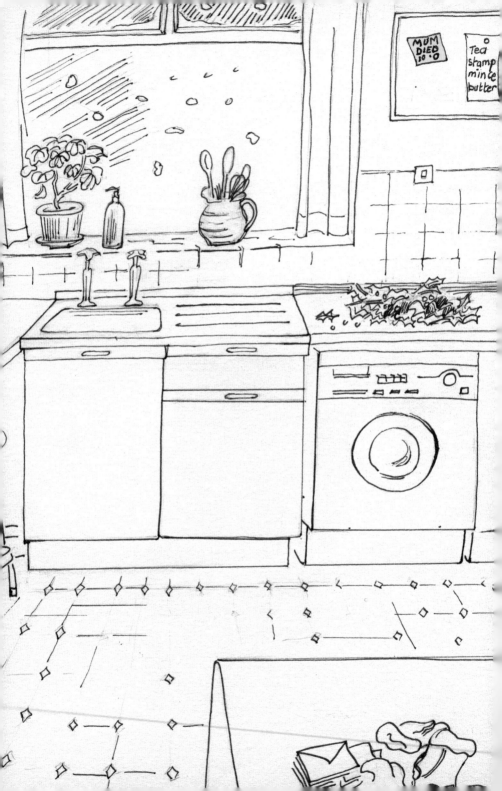

MUM
DIED
10 · 0

Tea
stamp
mince
butter

News of Her Death

Late evening, Christmas Day,
Phone ringing, message to say
She's dead, died suddenly.
Sad Post-it note of tragedy.

Yellow note adheres in pain,
Her death deserved more dignity.
Tell me quietly, calmly, kindly
Don't cheapen life so casually.

Sound of death's knell never kind.
Does not respect life's etiquette.
Like death itself, it rings to remind;
No call for complacency.

Just Miserable Awhile

Funeral now over, visitors all gone,
Close the door, feel all alone.
New life just beginning,
I can hear me moan.

Changing, changing, changing,
Everything has changed for me.
"I must tell her", "She's not there."
I must adjust my memory.

What's happened to my friends?
They treat me like a child.
Afraid to talk to me of her.
Don't tell me! "The weather's mild."

Only half of me is here now,
I lurch, unbalanced days.
Half my world has gone away.
I face uncharted ways.

All I want is sympathy
Your pity I don't need
I'm still alive, just talk to me.
Cold silence, cruelest deed.

And when you have to go,
Please promise to return.
Not next year, very soon,
I've such a lot to learn.

When I close the door on you,
The terrors will all loom.
You walk back to your cosy world,
I sink back to my tomb.

I'm sure one day you'll come again,
And see me with a smile.
I'm determined to begin again,
Just miserable awhile.

A Daughter Bids Farewell

A note before we go! To leave in memory.
Our feelings show in our sincerity.
So tired asleep now, fast asleep I see.
With dignity you bow, from cares set free.

We can smile now. Thoughts of earlier days
Remind us how you formed our ways.
Important in your eyes you made us seem.
Strong to realise ambition's dream.

Example you gave, authority and respect.
Wisdom you displayed, strength to correct.
As confidence grows in children who are sure,
Their mother knows, with her secure.

The Lord has wakened you from tiring days.
In life now rich and new, restored your gaze.
Has granted rest, given you true peace.
Your good life blessed, your worries cease.

Compassion

Compassion, suffering with another.
Ability to feel and mutually.
Accepted my pain, you suffered,
Lightened my load eventually.

Compassion, suffering shared
No empty words declared,
I know you cared.

Compassion, suffering together
The fear of being abused.
Now I have recovered,
I'm grateful you were there.

Children's Holocaust Memorial

Into the darkness of our lives
There shines the life of each dead child.
Blackness, darkness, death decreed
By men of hatred all defiled.

Each candle represents a life,
A flame that flickered then was spent.
Blackness, darkness, sin has reigned,
But their lives a message sent.

Their lives survive are not destroyed,
The light of their lives flickers on.
Blackness, darkness needs their light,
Need to learn or hope is gone.

Each one leaves the hall of lights
To face the light of their own lives.
Let the flicker of the candles burn.
Lesson learned? Then hope survives.

Hear the name of each dead child,
A name, a name, a life survives.
Their names must echo down the years,
Or nameless crime has cancelled lives.

Names will echo, echo names.
Candle flicker, burn the flames.
Darkness, blindness, disturbs, no rest!
The sin of humankind remains.

Out of My Depth

Out of my depth, I cry
To anyone but you O Lord!
You never listen to my prayer
Religion leaves me cold.

You were first port of call,
Safe harbour from the sea.
Storm came, where were you?
You just abandoned me!

Out of my depth, I cry
For friends to stand by me.
Some seemed to wonder why
I bothered them with grief.

One seemed to understand
In pain accepted me.
Listened, understood,
Slowly set me free.

Out of my depth, I cry.
God deaf, friend was there.
Why Lord, why not nigh?
Do you really care?

Why ask? I should know
God is no safety shield.
Is with us in our grief,
In true friends is revealed.

Perceive New Colours

All that gave colour to my life,
Brought rich variety to every day,
Was lost in loss. Now black and white,
Colours of life all drained away.

You saw the dullness in my gaze,
Glazed eyes downcast, sorrow's cost.
I saw my life in shades of grey,
Etched deep with scars of loss.

Your sympathy has cleared my sight,
Perceive new colours in the grey.
Stained glass windows recognise,
Held in the lead of long dark days.